TRENDS IN SOUTHEAST ASIA

The **ISEAS – Yusof Ishak Institute** (formerly Institute of Southeast Asian Studies) is an autonomous organization established in 1968. It is a regional centre dedicated to the study of socio-political, security, and economic trends and developments in Southeast Asia and its wider geostrategic and economic environment. The Institute's research programmes are grouped under Regional Economic Studies (RES), Regional Strategic and Political Studies (RSPS), and Regional Social and Cultural Studies (RSCS). The Institute is also home to the ASEAN Studies Centre (ASC), the Singapore APEC Study Centre and the Temasek History Research Centre (THRC).

ISEAS Publishing, an established academic press, has issued more than 2,000 books and journals. It is the largest scholarly publisher of research about Southeast Asia from within the region. ISEAS Publishing works with many other academic and trade publishers and distributors to disseminate important research and analyses from and about Southeast Asia to the rest of the world.

THE DEMOCRATIC ACTION PARTY IN JOHOR

Assailing the Barisan Nasional Fortress

Kevin Zhang, John Choo and Fong Sok Eng

ISSUE

17

2021

ISEAS YUSOF ISHAK INSTITUTE

Published by: ISEAS Publishing
30 Heng Mui Keng Terrace
Singapore 119614
publish@iseas.edu.sg
http://bookshop.iseas.edu.sg

ISEAS Library Cataloguing-in-Publication Data

Name(s): Zhang, Kevin, 1993–, author. | Choo, John, 1993–, author. | Fong, Sok Eng, 1993–, author.
Title: The Democratic Action Party in Johor : assailing the Barisan Nasional fortress / Kevin Zhang, John Choo and Fong Sok Eng.
Description: Singapore : ISEAS-Yusof Ishak Institute, October 2021. | Series: Trends in Southeast Asia, ISSN 0219-3213 ; TRS17/21 | Includes bibliographical references.
Identifiers: ISBN 9789815011104 (soft cover) | ISBN 9789815011111 (pdf)
Subjects: LCSH: Johor (Malaysia)—Politics and government. | Democratic Action Party. | Political parties—Malaysia—Johor.
Classification: LCC DS501 I59T no. 17(2021)

Typeset by Superskill Graphics Pte Ltd
Printed in Singapore by Mainland Press Pte Ltd

FOREWORD

The economic, political, strategic and cultural dynamism in Southeast Asia has gained added relevance in recent years with the spectacular rise of giant economies in East and South Asia. This has drawn greater attention to the region and to the enhanced role it now plays in international relations and global economics.

The sustained effort made by Southeast Asian nations since 1967 towards a peaceful and gradual integration of their economies has had indubitable success, and perhaps as a consequence of this, most of these countries are undergoing deep political and social changes domestically and are constructing innovative solutions to meet new international challenges. Big Power tensions continue to be played out in the neighbourhood despite the tradition of neutrality exercised by the Association of Southeast Asian Nations (ASEAN).

The **Trends in Southeast Asia** series acts as a platform for serious analyses by selected authors who are experts in their fields. It is aimed at encouraging policymakers and scholars to contemplate the diversity and dynamism of this exciting region.

THE EDITORS

Series Chairman:
    Choi Shing Kwok

Series Editor:
    Ooi Kee Beng

Editorial Committee:
    Daljit Singh
    Francis E. Hutchinson
    Norshahril Saat

The Democratic Action Party in Johor: Assailing the Barisan Nasional Fortress

By Kevin Zhang, John Choo and Fong Sok Eng

EXECUTIVE SUMMARY

- Until approximately two decades ago, the Democratic Action Party (DAP) struggled to make inroads in Johor due to: (1) the unique historical developments in the state, which benefited its primary opponent Barisan Nasional (BN), and (2) the decentralized party structure in Johor with party branches serving as the main player responsible for grassroots mobilization and campaigning, which resulted in an underdeveloped and less cohesive state party structure.

- Despite Lee Kaw playing a crucial leadership role for the nascent party to take root in the state, Johor remained in the periphery during the initial decades of the party's establishment. The party managed to achieve some electoral success only in central Johor around the Kluang.

- The party achieved a rare breakthrough in Johor during the 1990 General Election when numerous Chinese educationalists allied with the DAP under the call of then Dong Zong chairman Lim Fong Seng. However, the national alliance frayed soon after, with the DAP losing its momentum in Johor by the next general election.

- Dr Boo Cheng Hau inherited the decentralized state leadership structure when he became the DAP Johor chairman in 2005. Under Dr Boo's leadership the party prioritized welfare provision and constituency services in several state constituencies, particularly Skudai (in Gelang Patah) and Bentayan (in Bakri). The grassroots machinery was also strengthened while mechanisms were established to resolve intra-party conflicts in the lead-up to general elections.

- In the 2008 General Election, these efforts paid off and DAP Johor achieved its (till then) best results by capturing four state constituencies—including Skudai and Bentayan—in addition to the Bakri parliamentary seat.
- In the aftermath of GE2008, where DAP made unprecedented gains in Penang, Selangor and Perak, the national DAP leadership began to shift their attention towards Johor as the latter was perceived as the next frontline state. The party continued its upward swing and made unprecedented gains in the 2013 General Election.
- As DAP maintained its momentum, coupled with the success of other Pakatan Harapan (PH) component parties in Johor during the 2018 General Election, the DAP under the PH coalition displaced BN as the Johor state government.

The Democratic Action Party in Johor: Assailing the Barisan Nasional Fortress

By Kevin Zhang, John Choo and Fong Sok Eng[1]

SITUATING JOHOR DAP WITHIN MALAYSIAN POLITICS

In the 2018 General Election (GE2018), the Democratic Action Party (DAP) made an almost clean sweep in Johor. Except for the Ayer Hitam parliamentary constituency, DAP captured all the other six parliamentary and fourteen state constituencies it contested in the state. Apart from the United Malays National Organization (UMNO), the DAP had the second-highest number of state assembly seats in GE2018. After several UMNO Johor state assemblymen defected to Parti Pribumi Bersatu Malaysia (PPBM), the DAP and UMNO presently have an equal number of representatives in the state assembly, at fourteen each. Being a key component member of Pakatan Harapan (PH) coalition, the DAP was part of the PH state administration which governed Johor from GE2018 until the Sheraton Move in February 2020. The rise of DAP in Johor in 2018 is exceptional, as the party for most part of its history, was not a significant political force in the state.

---

[1] Kevin Zhang, John Choo and Fong Sok Eng are Research Officers at the ISEAS – Yusof Ishak Institute, Singapore. Kevin Zhang is with the Malaysia Studies Programme; John Choo was an assistant (2018–20) for the Social Science Research Thematic Grant (SSRTG) project "Christianity in Southeast Asia: Comparative Growth, Politics and Networks in Urban Centres"; and Fong Sok Eng is with the Archaeology Unit. The authors would like to thank Francis Hutchinson, Lee Hwok Aun and Liew Chin Tong for their helpful comments on earlier drafts, and Rebecca Neo for creating the GIS maps.

Demographics of Johor

Johor serves as an interesting case for the DAP as the state has a demographic composition that is similar to Penang's and Selangor's in terms of a sizeable Chinese population. Johoreans of Chinese descent constitute 34 per cent of the overall population, compared to Penang (46 per cent) and Kuala Lumpur (43 per cent). With a population of 3.75 million, Johor is the third most populous state in Malaysia, and only a notch below Sabah.[2] The share of Johoreans residing in urban areas closely mirrors the national average of 71 per cent.[3] However, in contrast to the significant support the DAP had had in Penang, Selangor and Perak since 1969, the party had not been able to replicate that success in Johor (Table 1). Even before the 2008 General Election (GE2008) which

Table 1: Seats Won by the DAP in the 1969 General Election

	Parliamentary	State
Selangor	3	9
Perak	5	6
Penang	1	3
Johor	0	1

Source: Stuart Drummond and David Hawkins, "The Malaysian Elections of 1969: An Analysis of the Campaign and the Results", *Asian Survey* 10, no. 4 (1970): 329.

---

[2] See Statistics Department Malaysia, https://www.dosm.gov.my/v1/index.php?r=column/cone&menu_id=d1dTR0JMK2hUUUFnTnp5WUR2d3VBQT09 (accessed 24 June 2021).

[3] See Statistics Department Malaysia, https://www.dosm.gov.my/v1/index.php?r=column/ctheme&menu_id=L0pheU43NWJwRWVSZklWdzQ4TlhUUT09&bul_id=MDMxdHZjWTk1SjFzTzNkRXYzcVZjdz09 (accessed 25 June 2021).

denied Barisan Nasional (BN) its customary two-thirds parliamentary majority, the DAP was typically able to gain a commendable number of parliament and state seats in Penang, Selangor and Perak. The same could not be said of Johor.

Johor is politically significant to Malaysia's national politics for having the second-highest number of parliamentary seats among Malaysian states, behind Sarawak. Coincidentally, the state government in Johor has always been aligned to the federal government in Putrajaya, be it during the Alliance/BN era (1957–2018), the PH government (2018–20), the Perikatan Nasional (2020–21), or the present administration led by Prime Minister Ismail Sabri.

Aside from the blip in 1990, the DAP began to make inroads into Johor only since GE2008. However, within a decade it has become a formidable contender—in a state long-considered as the bastion of BN. This article seeks to understand why the DAP failed to make inroads into Johor for the most part of the party's history, as well as its exponential rise since GE2008.

LITERATURE REVIEW

Existing Literature Has Given Scant Attention to DAP in Johor

Existing academic literature on the DAP has concentrated on key leaders within the party, including party veteran Lim Kit Siang and Karpal Singh.[4] While some scholars have written about the party's internal structure, the focus has either been at the national level or on states where the DAP is strong (e.g., Selangor and Penang), and scant attention has been given

---

[4] See Ooi Kee Beng, *Lim Kit Siang: Defying the Odds* (Singapore: Marshall Cavendish, 2015); Ooi Kee Beng, *The Right to Differ: A Biographical Sketch of Lim Kit Siang* (Kuala Lumpur: Research for Social Advancement, 2011); Lim Kit Siang and Wong Shu Qi, *Malaysia's Time Bomb: Lit Kit Siang 50 Years in Politics Chinese Edition (馬來西亞的計時炸彈: 林吉祥從政50周年中文紀念版)* (Kuala Lumpur: Genta Media, 2015); Tim Donoghue, *Karpal Singh: Tiger of Jelutong* (Singapore: Marshall Cavendish, 2013).

to the DAP in Johor.[5] At the same time, the political literature for Johor has been almost exclusively on BN—particularly for UMNO and the Malaysian Chinese Association (MCA)—due to its stellar performance up till the 2013 General Election (GE2013).[6] Situated on the opposite ends of the political spectrum, the fortunes of the DAP in Johor can be argued to be inversely related to the performance of BN. The strength of UMNO and MCA in Johor provides an important—though not complete—picture to account for the DAP's relative underperformance in the state during the initial decades of the party's formation.

Strength of UMNO and MCA Due to Unique Historical Developments in Johor

Under the Malaysian consociational model of politics, each ethnic group was represented by their respective elites which comprised the various race-based parties within the ruling Alliance Party or Barisan Nasional coalition (1957 to 2018).[7] UMNO champions for the interests of ethnic Malays, while the Malaysian Chinese Association (MCA) and the Malaysian Indian Congress (MIC) seek to represent the interests of Chinese and Indians, respectively. The strength of BN in Johor,

---

[5] See Hew Kuan Yau, *A Study of DAP: Beyond Dogmatism and Pragmatism (超越教条与务实: 马来西亚民主行动党研究)* (Selangor: Mentor Publishing, 2007); Harold Crouch, *Malaysia's 1982 General Elections* (Singapore: Institute of Southeast Asian Studies, 1982); Satish Kumar, "Democratic Action Party in Malaysian Political Scenario: 1966–1978" (BA thesis, National University of Singapore, 1979); Andy Mickey Choong, "Democratic Action Party of Malaysia and the Politics of Opposition Coalition Building" (MSc thesis, National University of Singapore, 2006).

[6] See Francis Hutchinson, *GE-14 in Johor: The Fall of the Fortress?* Trends in Southeast Asia, no. 3/2018 (Singapore: ISEAS – Yusof Ishak Institute, 2018); Lee Hock Guan and Nicholas Chan, *Electoral Politics and The Malaysian Chinese Association in Johor*, Trends in Southeast Asia, no. 20/2018 (Singapore: ISEAS – Yusof Ishak Institute, 2018).

[7] Francis E. Hutchinson, "UMNO and Barisan Nasional in Johor", in *Johor: An Abode of Development?* edited by Francis E. Hutchinson and Serina Rahman (Singapore: ISEAS – Yusof Ishak Institute, 2020), p. 217.

however, stems from consociationalism where the collective strength of the coalition is based on the agglomeration of each component party.[8] In Johor, UMNO and MCA held the bulk of parliamentary and state seats, and the state remained both these parties' impregnable fortress till the early 2000s.

Until the last decade, Johor was a stronghold for UMNO with the state historically playing an essential role in the party's formation and subsequent growth. UMNO was founded during the immediate post-war years as numerous Malay groups came together to oppose the Malayan Union plan proposed by the British.[9] Several key national UMNO leaders came from Johor, including the party's founder and first president Onn Jaafar, who also served as Johor Chief Minister between 1947 and 1950. Hussein Onn, Malaysia's third Prime Minister and UMNO president during 1978–81, was similarly a Johorean who represented the Sri Gading constituency seat. Other prominent Johoreans include Musa Hitam, who served as the country's Deputy Prime Minister from 1981 to 1986 and represented numerous constituencies in Johor during his career. As Johoreans rose up the ranks of national leadership, they further cemented the organizational capacity and machinery of UMNO Johor.

UMNO also benefited from a unique demographic advantage in Johor which is less salient in other states save Pahang. Johor has the second-largest number of Federal Land Development Agency (FELDA) settlers,[10] and FELDA communities are overwhelmingly favourable towards UMNO as the scheme provides landless (and low-income) bumiputra with grants and land to produce agricultural crops.[11] Upon being resettled in FELDA estates, residents are typically able to fetch a higher income compared to their previous position as a sharecropper.[12]

---

[8] Ibid., p. 219.

[9] Ibid., p. 223.

[10] Ibid., p. 228.

[11] Only very few FELDA settlements were open to non-bumiputra Malaysians.

[12] James C. Scott, *Weapons of the Weak: Everyday Forms of Peasant Resistance* (New Haven: Yale University Press, 1985).

Despite FELDA being a scheme under the federal government, the UMNO party machinery often played a key role in the selection of settlers and disbursement of resettlement grants.[13] UMNO grassroots in FELDA settlements, particularly in Johor, also managed the social aspects of the community including Islamic prayer sessions. Under these circumstances, the DAP faced a great challenge in making inroads into Malay-majority constituencies in Johor.

As DAP typically contests under an opposition alliance, it could depend on its coalition partners in certain states. However, this strategy was not viable in Johor as UMNO faced little opposition from its main rival, the Malaysian Islamic Party (Parti Islam Se-Malaysia, or PAS). PAS, being the sole alternative Malay-based party (at least prior to the formation of PPBM in 2016), posed the greatest threat to UMNO nationally. Despite its formidable base in the east coast states on the peninsula, it had not been able to gain a foothold in Johor due to differences in Islamic ideologies between PAS and Johorean Malays. PAS is influenced by modernist Islamic teachings while Johor religious authorities are traditionalists.[14] PAS is generally not well received among Johorean Malays, and strict regulations from the Johor Islamic religious department effectively prohibit PAS from establishing Islamic boarding schools (pondok) in Johor, unlike the case in other states on the peninsula.[15]

While ineffective in wrestling Malay-majority constituencies from UMNO in Johor, the DAP had not been able to achieve much success either in securing Chinese-majority or mixed constituencies in Johor until recently. These seats were mostly held by BN component parties

---

[13] Ibid.

[14] Wan Saiful Wan Jan, *PAS: Unifier of the Ummah?* Trends in Southeast Asia, no. 14/2020 (Singapore: ISEAS – Yusof Ishak Institute, 2020), p. 17; Norshahril Saat, *Johor Remains the Bastion of Kaum Tua*, Trends in Southeast Asia, no. 1/2017 (Singapore: ISEAS – Yusof Ishak Institute, 2017).

[15] Hutchinson, "UMNO and Barisan Nasional in Johor", p. 226.

save for a few under UMNO, with MCA being the largest player for Chinese-majority and mixed constituencies.

Compared to Perak, Penang and Selangor where ethnic Chinese are concentrated in a few constituencies, the Chinese population is relatively dispersed across Johor.[16] Furthermore while Perak, Selangor and Penang respectively have two, one and three Chinese supermajority (i.e., share of Chinese exceeding 70 per cent of the electorate) parliamentary seats, Johor has none. A similar pattern is observed in state seats; Johor has fewer Chinese supermajority seats than the three states. Consequently, the Malay community constitutes a significant share of the electorate in the mixed and Chinese-majority seats contested by MCA, at both parliament and state assembly level in Johor. Due to vote pooling among BN component parties and solid support among Malays in Johor for BN (until the recent decade), MCA had performed better in Johor than Perak, Selangor and Penang.

However, the strength of MCA in Johor goes beyond demographics and extends into unique historical developments in the state. MCA has the advantage of a strong grassroots machinery in Johor which had ties with local governmental agencies and Chinese guilds and associations (CGAs). Beginning in the 1800s, the Kangchu system, instituted by then Johor ruler Daeng Ibrahim, provided Chinese immigrants the right to cultivate land in exchange for taxation revenue.[17] Johor has the second-highest number of New Villages created during the Communist Insurgency, after Perak. MCA played an important role in the provision of amenities and welfare when New Villages were first established in Johor, in collaboration with CGAs.[18]

---

[16] Lee and Chan, *Electoral Politics and The Malaysian Chinese Association in Johor*, p. 20.

[17] *The Edge*, "GE 13 DAP Veteran Says Chinese in Johor 'No Longer Indebted'", 3 May 2013, https://www.theedgemarkets.com/article/ge13-dap-veteran-says-chinese-johor-no-longer-indebted (accessed 24 June 2021).

[18] Lee and Chan, *Electoral Politics and The Malaysian Chinese Association in Johor*, pp. 14–15.

Since the ministerial portfolio for Housing and Local Government was traditionally reserved for the MCA, the party wielded significant influence in the appointment of village security and development committees (JKKK) and village chiefs.[19] MCA members in Johor came to dominate New Villages Committees and Local Councils, which in turn accorded them the authority to allocate licences and land rights.[20] The Group Settlement Areas (GSA) land scheme—under the Land (Group Settlement Areas) Act 1960—permitted Malaysians including those classified as non-bumiputra to acquire new agricultural land, and till the late 1980s the Johor state government offered new land to Johorean Chinese after each general election.[21] Rural residents were generally eager to apply for the land scheme since they could increase their agricultural produce (mainly oil palm) and fetch a higher income. Though the scheme was theoretically eligible to all Malaysians, the MCA in practice only processed land applications for residents in polling districts which BN had won.[22] Until 1980, the majority of Johorean Chinese resided in rural areas and, through its involvement in key local affairs and land permits, MCA gained a huge electoral advantage against the DAP.

RESEARCH METHODOLOGY

Primary Data Collection Through Interviews

Due to scarce academic writings for the DAP in Johor as well as a lack of party archival documents, the authors conducted an extensive data collection from both primary and secondary sources. For primary data

---

[19] Local elections were suspended in the 1960s due to the communist insurgency and have not revived. Local councillors and village chiefs are political appointees decided by the incumbent state administration.

[20] Lee Hock Guan and Nicholas Chan, "Electoral Politics and the Malaysian Chinese Association in Johor", in *Johor: An Abode of Development?* edited by Francis E. Hutchinson and Serina Rahman (Singapore: ISEAS – Yusof Ishak Institute, 2020), p. 245.

[21] Ibid.

[22] *The Edge*, "GE 13 DAP Veteran Says Chinese in Johor 'No Longer Indebted'".

collection, physical and online interviews (due to movement restrictions) were conducted with sixteen DAP members from Johor. Interviews are particularly useful when the events recounted are not documented by the press or party archive, and for revealing the participants' perspectives. Most of the sixteen are presently serving or have once served as elected representatives—either as Johor state assemblyperson or parliamentarians. The remaining three are long-time grassroots members in DAP Johor (see Appendix 1 for the list of interviewees). Most of the interviewees also sat on the DAP Johor state committee—the highest decision-making body in the state—at various periods, with some serving the party in the 1970s. To gather sentiments directly from grassroots and party members, one of the authors attended the DAP Johor state convention held in 2018.

Secondary Data Collection through English and Chinese Print Media Archives and Granular Election Results at the Polling District Level

Secondary sources are also necessary to complement and corroborate the research findings. Drawing from Malaysian (and to a lesser extent Singaporean) English and Chinese print media outlets, news archives also served as a valuable source of secondary data in addition to academic resources such as books and journals. English and Chinese print media outlets consulted include *Sin Chew Daily, Nanyang Siang Pao, New Straits Times* and *Lianhe Zaobao*. Past-election results were also analysed stretching back to 1969. One author also visited the Center for Malaysian Chinese Studies in Kuala Lumpur to access archival materials that are not reported in the media. Granular election data, at the polling district or Pusat Daerah Mengundi (PDM), are also analysed to understand voting patterns among ethnic groups.

Prior to the early 2000s, the DAP was underdeveloped in Johor and the periodization is based on splits or alliances within the party national leadership. The most prominent schisms during the period were the Goh Hock Guan episode (1972) and Chan Teck Chan episode (1981), while the alliance between Chinese educationalist Dong Zong top leaders and the DAP (1990) was a high point for the party. While the Goh-Lim dispute had little impact on the DAP in Johor, the expulsion of Chan and the alliance with Dong Zong created significant ripple effects in the party in the state.

Hence the periodization before the 2000s is as follows, and the subsequent sections will deal with each in turn:

- 1966–69: Establishment of DAP in Malaysia with the first seeds sowed in Johor
- 1970–74: Lim Kit Siang takes over with the departure of Goh Hock Guan
- 1975–84: Chan Teck Chan expelled from the party
- 1985–99: DAP allies with Chinese educationalist Dong Zong and the subsequent fallout

1966-69: TRYING TIMES

With the separation of Singapore from Malaysia in 1965, PAP branches in Malaysia had to quickly re-establish themselves within the new political climate. Initially, party leaders proposed the name "PAP Malaya" but the title was rejected by the Registrar of Societies (ROS). Finally, DAP was chosen and its registration was allowed.

The DAP in Johor started in a disadvantageous position. Since 1964, as part of federal policy in the country's *Konfrontasi* with Indonesia, local government elections had been suspended across Malaysia. The urban councils in Johor Bahru and Batu Pahat were abolished altogether in April and May 1966, respectively, months prior to the establishment of the DAP.[23] There were few opportunities for the party, already hampered by the departure of its Singapore sponsors following the expulsion of the island-state from the Federation in August 1965, to till the ground for grassroots support. Hence, despite the party's efforts to burnish its

---

[23] Paul Tennant, "The Decline of Elective Local Government in Malaysia", *Asian Survey* 13, no. 4 (1973), pp. 348 and 352; Chew Huat Hock, "The Democratic Action Party in Post-1969 Malaysian Politics: The Strategy of a Determined Opposition" (MA thesis, Australian National University, 1980), p. 53.

socialist credentials through joining the Socialist International in October 1967 and establishing a Labour Bureau in April 1968, its appeal was limited.

During the DAP's inaugural national party dinner in July 1966, party chairman Chen Man Hin, who had entered the Negeri Sembilan state legislature as an independent a year before, rallied members around the cause of democratic socialism, echoing the final cries of the PAP before it left the peninsula. He told those present that the ideology could bring about a broad-based, non-racial movement that would eradicate exploitation of all sorts.[24] In an attempt to exemplify the seriousness with which it took its project, the DAP established seven branches by the end of the year, with three of them headed by a non-Chinese chairman.

One of these was in Johor Bahru, where the post was given to medical doctor K.S. Das, assisted by secretary Mohd Nor bin Jettey. Both men were part of the first Central Executive Committee (CEC).[25] Yet, this did not constitute the formation of a state-level organizational apparatus in Johor. Even when the state committee was created, it was a largely ceremonial affair. Recruitment and electoral deployment decisions were made primarily using the discretion of members of the central leadership, based on the recommendations of their own personal networks. Outside of these spheres, candidates were left to their own devices, especially when it came to developing their campaign strategy and tactics. This arrangement in Johor meant that electoral success in these nascent years was extremely dependent on the abilities of individuals, rather than on what the party could offer at the time.

Given Johor's inhospitable terrain, filling the party's ranks thus required tapping on people who were known quantities in the local political scene. Born in Batu Pahat, then-national organizing secretary Lim Kit Siang was one of the better-placed in those years to scout for talent. It was he who brought onboard some of DAP Johor's earliest

---

[24] Democratic Action Party, *25 Years of Struggle: Milestones in DAP History* (Petaling Jaya: DAP, 1991), pp. 2–3.

[25] Ibid., p. 4.

stalwarts. One of the first state chairmen, Lee Ah Meng, was a leader of the Oversea-Chinese Banking Corporation (OCBC) bankers' union, while the Batu Pahat chairperson was a friend of Lim's.[26] Another DAP state chairman-to-be Lee Kaw was introduced to Lim by Labour Party of Malaya (LPM) secretary-general Wee Lee Fong, during the time Lim served as political secretary to the first DAP secretary-general Devan Nair. These connections bred others; for example, Lee Kaw would join the party alongside ex-LPM Segamat secretary K. Siladass, who would in turn induct Krishna Nair Raman, the 1969 DAP candidate for Rengam.[27]

At this point in time, though, these membership chains were not integrated into a single DAP Johor unit, but instead reported separately to Lim. Party branches, insofar as these acquaintance clusters could be called such, were generally unaware of each other's activities. Those operating in Kluang, for example, were not expected to know what was happening in Johor Bahru, and vice versa.[28]

Johor was the site for what were only the second and third by-elections contested by the young DAP. With the active involvement of the CEC, these contests demonstrated the party's determination to realize its vision of an alternative multiethnic Malaysia from that fashioned by the Alliance government. They were also risky battles, fought at the doorstep of UMNO, the lead partner of the Alliance. In September 1967, the party fielded CEC member Daing Ibrahim Othman to fight for a place in the state legislature in Tampoi, following the death of UMNO member Daud Ahmad. A year later, in October, it pitted Lee Ah Meng against UMNO executive secretary and future Deputy Prime Minister Musa Hitam in the Segamat Utara parliamentary constituency. Devan Nair and Chen Man Hin gave rally speeches for the former,[29] whilst new secretary-general

---

[26] Lee Kaw, personal correspondence, 19 November 2020.

[27] K. Siladass, personal correspondence, 24 November 2020.

[28] Lee Kaw, ibid.; K. Siladass, ibid.

[29] *Straits Times*, "DAP Fires the First Shots", 6 September 1967, p. 13.

Goh Hock Guan and Lim Kit Siang were present at the latter.[30] The risks did not pay off.

When the May 1969 general elections were held, the DAP under Goh and Lim decided to intensify the party's call for a "Malaysian Malaysia", framed as the inverse of what it controversially termed the Alliance's "Malay Malaysia".[31] In Johor, it continued with the deployment strategy of training its biggest guns on UMNO, with Daing Ibrahim Othman and Lee Ah Meng returning to face Mohamed Rahmat and future Prime Minister Hussein Onn in the Johor Bahru Barat and Johor Bahru Timor parliamentary constituencies respectively.

Perhaps due to the nationwide scale of the elections, as compared to the two by-elections, DAP Johor candidates were mostly unsupported by party infrastructure this time. They were only given a stack of party posters and a printer's address, having to arrange and pay for their photographs to be affixed to them on their own dime. They also had to recruit canvassers on their own.[32] In the absence of a state-level coordinating body, the neglect of the party's central leadership was keenly felt.

Consequently, it was up to the unique resourcefulness of Lee Kaw to provide the DAP with its sole victory in Johor, of the six parliamentary and twelve state assembly seats contested by the party. Having been the Kluang-based logistics provider for the LPM and the PAP in the 1950s and early 1960s, as well as the boss of a local petrochemical supply shop, Lee was able to tap on a wide acquaintance and employee network for support. On top of that, K. Siladass was able to put him in touch with members of the Indian community, expanding his popular reach to a degree.[33] It was enough to narrowly beat the MCA's Siew Theng Yhoi by 1,104 votes in the Gunung Lambak state assembly contest, but

---

[30] Lee Kaw, ibid.; K. Siladass, ibid.

[31] Sothi Rachagan, "The 1974 Parliamentary Election in Peninsular Malaysia: A Study in Electoral Geography" (PhD thesis, School of Oriental and African Studies, 1978), p. 227; Chew, "The Democratic Action Party", pp. 3–4.

[32] Lee Kaw, ibid.

[33] Ibid.

insufficient to capture the larger Kluang Utara parliamentary seat held by the MCA's Tiah Eng Bee, of which Gunung Lambak was a part. Lee would go on to serve as Johor's sole opposition representative until 1982. Unlike other states (see Table 1), DAP failed to make inroads into Johor apart from capturing the Gunung Lambak state seat.

Three days after the elections, race riots between ethnic Chinese and Malays erupted in Malaysia's capital, sparked by victory parades held by the DAP and the Gerakan Rakyat Malaysia. Chinese party supporters were reported to have insulted Malay policemen and residents, calling them to return to their villages, among other cries.[34] The country was thrust into a state of emergency and Prime Minister Tunku Abdul Rahman was eventually forced to resign. Partial blame was assigned to the DAP's national electoral message, paving the way for a time of self-reflection and infighting.

1970–74: A NEW NATIONAL LEADERSHIP

In the immediate aftermath of the May 13 incident, Lim Kit Siang was detained for eighteen months under the Internal Security Act (ISA), for having allegedly roused communalist feelings that allegedly fuelled the disorder. Goh Hock Guan, in contrast, was understood to have left the country, and was attending the Socialist International Conference in London and visiting several other European governments, purportedly to convince foreign politicians to place pressure on the provisional National Operations Council (NOC) for Lim's release.[35] Five months later, Lim succeeded Goh to become the DAP's secretary-general. A bitter and personal conflict between these two party leaders would

---

[34] *Straits Times*, "Brinkmanship on Racial Issues—And Step by Step to May 13 Riots", 9 October 1969, p. 1.

[35] *Straits Times*, "I Do Not Wish to Associate with Lim: Goh", 19 June 1972, p. 31; *Straits Times*, "Revolt Threat by Four DAP Branches", 11 July 1972, p. 9; Raymond Chong, "Loyal Veteran: Interview with Former DAP Perak Chairman and ISA detainee Lau Dak Kee", *The Rocket*, 9 June 2014, https://www.therocket.com.my/en/lau-dak-kees-reflections-with-the-dap/

unfold in ensuing years, becoming a template for similar leadership tussles that would arise in later decades. Nevertheless, Lim's previous role as the main party liaison in Johor, coupled with the state party's decentralized structure, prevented the DAP in the state from being too adversely affected by Goh's eventual exit in 1972, despite the state being one of the primary backdrops for the disagreement. However, partly because of emergency restrictions, the party was unable to capitalize on the loyalty of its members to strengthen its organization. It drifted along unchanged.

A facet of the Lim-Goh conflict concerned tactics. After his arrest, Lim Kit Siang convinced the party to step up its belligerent attitude against the government, extending the scope of its critique further than before. At a 1971 DAP congress, he denounced the existence of the ISA, a reversal from the party's 1967 Setapak Declaration that offered cautious assent.[36] In the same year, he vigorously opposed the Constitutional (Amendment) Bill that restricted open discussion on matters deemed by the state to be in the interest of security or public order. This was widely construed as a reckless position to take, particularly as Gerakan president and fellow opposition member Lim Chong Eu depicted the bill in patriotic terms, as being "for the survival of Malaysia and against the enemies of our nation".[37] Lim's new approach thus had internal detractors. In December 1970, former Muar branch chairman, failed Kluang Selatan parliamentary candidate, and Johor state organizing secretary Lee Kuo Ming condemned the party as "racialist" and "detrimental to a multi-racial democratic Malaysia".[38] He left to join Gerakan.

Unlike others within the DAP, Goh Hock Guan did not appear to oppose Lim Kit Siang's methods in principle. Instead, he purportedly sought to carve his own path of operations, independent of Lim's oversight. The incident that triggered his departure from the party, after

---

[36] Chew, "The Democratic Action Party", pp. 83–84.

[37] Cited in *Straits Times*, "Gerakan Leader Backs Bill", 2 March 1971, p. 1.

[38] Noordin Sopiee, "Decline of the DAP: The Reasons Why ...", *Straits Times*, 11 July 1972, p. 12.

all, was Goh's public divergence from the party line on the government's plans to internationalize the Strait of Malacca.

The populace, nonetheless, already had a glimpse of these internal divisions in Johor in July 1971. It was leaked to the press that three months prior, Goh had entertained three secret meetings with MCA president Tan Siew Sin, mediated by future MCA president Lee San Choon and Chinese Unity Movement leader Alex Lee. Tan had tried to persuade the DAP to concede a Johor state assembly by-election in Bekok, where new DAP Muar branch chairman Chian Heng Kai faced MCA Paloh strongman Ng Nam Seng, as a precursor to a merger between the parties. Ministerial and party leadership positions were also proposed as part of the compact. This was framed as a banding together of ethnic Chinese politicians, necessary to stave off racial polarization in the country.[39] Even though it was acknowledged across the board that Chen Man Hin and Lim were subsequently made aware of the talks, with the two rejecting the MCA offer out of hand alongside Goh, accounts diverge as to whether they were informed of the conversations beforehand.[40]

The event was a source of negative attention for the DAP. As more details emerged that the MCA had, at an even earlier moment in time, made an aborted attempt to strike a deal with Lim Kit Siang,[41] some non-Chinese members of the party were stunned, interpreting the goings-on

---

[39] *Straits Times*, "Row Rages on Over MCA-DAP Secret Talks", 12 July 1971, p. 26; *Sin Chew Daily*, "Alex Lee Reveals That the Reason for MCA-DAP Talks Was the Need for Chinese Political Unity" (李裕隆披露与民行党会談原因認爲華籍從政人士需要團結), 12 July 1971, p. 9; *Sin Chew Daily*, "Goh Hock Guan Reveals That in Talks, Tan Siew Sin Offered DAP Leaders All MCA Leadership Positions" (吳福源揭露陈修仗曾在談判中獻議全部馬華職位交換民行黨魁入會), 12 July 1971, p. 9.

[40] Pakir Singh, "DAP Battle Enters Second Round: The Party Will Be the Ultimate Loser", *New Nation*, 22 June 1972, p. 8; *Sin Chew Daily*, "Goh Hock Guan Rebuts Lim Kit Siang's Account of Secret Talks with Tun Tan" (吳福源駁斥林吉祥曾與敦陳秘密會談), 22 June 1972, p. 9.

[41] *Sin Chew Daily*, "Lim Kit Siang Issues Clarification; Unity Talks Were Initiated by Tan Siew Sin" (林吉祥發表文告澄清聯邦協會內會談係陳修信先提議), 11 July 1971, p. 9.

as evidence of hypocrisy. When he joined Goh in quitting the DAP, the party's national vice-president and parliamentary whip A. Soorian called the party's adherence to multi-racialism a myth, accusing it of being "chauvinistic" in light of the leaked talks.[42] Spearheading the grassroots revolt in Selangor following Goh and Soorian's departure, Brickfields branch secretary Samuel Raj added to the attack by asking why party leaders had ignored the Malay and Tamil languages in their publicity materials.[43] The loss of trust among the non-Chinese party faithful seemingly spread to Johor as well. About a week and a half before Polling Day in August 1974, the DAP state assembly candidate for Buloh Kasap, Ali Mohamed Dom, suddenly declared that he was withdrawing from the electoral race. Pledging support for the newly formed Barisan Nasional (BN) under Prime Minister Tun Abdul Razak, he rejected the DAP for being an unhelpful presence with regard to the achievement of multi-racial peace.[44]

Still, the overall damage wrought by the party upheaval was minimal in the state, as most members were more familiar with Lim than with either Goh or Soorian.[45] They were struggling with a more serious problem, that of ensuring the viability of the state party itself. In accordance with the powers conferred on the NOC in 1969, the Essential (Prohibition of Activities Relating to Elections) Regulations were rolled out. All outreach activities were suspended, including visitations, public meetings, printing and distribution of political material, and press statements, essentially freezing the party in time.[46]

---

[42] *Straits Times*, "I Do Not Wish to Associate with Lim: Goh"; *Sin Chew Daily*, "DAP Leadership Officially Splits: Goh Hock Guan and Soorian to Leave Party" (民行黨領導層正式鬧分裂吳福源蘇里安退黨), 19 June 1972, p. 9.

[43] *Straits Times*, "Revolt Threat by Four DAP Branches".

[44] *Sin Chew Daily*, "Johor Buloh Kasap DAP candidate Ali Announces Withdrawal from the Party and the Election" (柔浮羅加什区州會候选人民行黨阿里宣佈退黨並放棄競選), 14 August 1974, p. 9.

[45] K. Siladass, ibid.

[46] *Malaysia: Ordinance No. 1 of 1969, Emergency (Essential Powers) Ordinance*, 15 May 1969, https://www.refworld.org/docid/3ae6b5604.html

In the lead-up to the 1974 general elections, key Johor personnel were transferred out of the state, preventing potential ideas for party improvement on a local level from being implemented once the regulations were lifted. In 1973, Kluang operative K. Siladass had decided to pursue a law degree in the United Kingdom,[47] and DAP Johor chairman Daing Ibrahim Othman, promoted to national vice-president, was redeployed to the federal constituency of Beruas and state assembly constituency of Pasir Puteh in Perak. Chian Heng Kai was likewise sent to Perak, to contest the federal Batu Gajah seat. The result at the end of the period was a mere retention of Lee Kaw's state assembly seat, renamed Bandar Kluang.

1975–84: THE BEGINNINGS OF CONSOLIDATION AND FRAGMENTATION

On 7 December 1974, Lee Kaw was announced as the new DAP Johor chairman, aided by state secretary Quek Swee Siang.[48] Lee was to become the longest-serving chairman that the state party would have. Under his leadership, the DAP in Johor matured. Local branches were more deeply institutionalized, serving as independent buttresses for electoral candidates, rather than just extensions of their social and professional circles. The state committee also began to have a larger role in the life of the party. Even so, the party remained highly decentralized, rendering it vulnerable to the growing rift between English-educated and Chinese-educated members within its midst, a microcosm of national party trends. Tentative steps were further taken to shift the party's electoral strategy, from contesting in competitive Malay-dominant seats to working with allied opposition parties that were perceived to have a higher chance of wrestling those seats from BN control. Situated as it was in an

---

[47] Wan Hamidi Hamid, "Interview with K. Siladass", *The Rocket*, 9 June 2014, https://www.therocket.com.my/en/siladass/

[48] *Sin Chew Daily*, "New Line-up for DAP Johor Branch" (民主行動黨柔分部新阵容产生), 7 December 1974, p. 11.

intermediate stage of transformation, the party would not yet bear much electoral fruit.

When Lee Kaw took the helm of DAP Johor, local branches developed to such an extent that they were the main initiators of fund-raising dinners and other canvassing activities. Given more elaborate electorally relevant undertakings, the state committee then had to take on responsibilities that it did not previously have, from showing up as patrons to branch events to organizing monthly statewide meetings. The agenda of these latter meetings revolved around the resolution of branch disputes and the introduction of members that branches wished to field as electoral candidates.[49] Although this novel system allowed for faster growth for the state party than before, reliance on the discretion of local branches inevitably opened the party up to infiltration by opportunistic profiteers and ambitious leadership aspirants. There were common worries that candidates-to-be would use the party's authorizing letter, presented to the returning officer on Nomination Day, as a bargaining chip for a financial settlement with the BN. For a price, they would concede walkovers.[50] Some DAP members were suspected of being Special Branch informers.[51]

In this environment where multiple sets of relational ties, some invisible to DAP leadership, superseded plainly articulated criteria for party promotion, one Chan Teck Chan swiftly rose up the ranks. Joining the party in 1971 as a volunteer in Kluang, he was first ushered deeper into the party fold as a potential replacement for Lee Kaw in his state assembly seat. Catching the eye of the DAP national leadership, he was soon catapulted to Malacca to serve as the Tranquerah state representative for the term beginning in 1974. Three short years later, he would be one of three new members of the CEC, serving as the deputy organizing secretary together with Lee, now a fellow inductee

---

[49] Lee Kaw, ibid.

[50] Ibid.

[51] Ibid.

and national treasurer.[52] He would be elected member of parliament for Kota Melaka in 1978, and director of the party's political bureau in 1979.[53]

In 1981, Chan was expelled, accused of breaching party discipline by allying with the Gang of Three in DAP Penang, namely, Seow Hun Khim, Chin Nyok Soo and Goh Lim Eam. They had assumed the mantle of speaking on behalf of Chinese-educated members, to denounce the supposed condescension and marginalization efforts of the party's English-educated leaders.[54] In sharp contrast to the departure of Goh and Soorian, due to Chan's early years cultivating friendships in Johor, at least two batches of party members from six branches, totalling around 115 people, quit in solidarity, possibly contributing to the party's loss of the Bandar Kluang state and the Kluang parliamentary seats in 1982.[55] In one of the press conferences where these members made their final statements, it was alleged that unpleasant interactions with then state secretary Lim Kwi Siam and other English-educated state committee

---

[52] *Sin Chew Daily*, "Chen Man Hin and Lim Kit Siang Re-elected as DAP Chairman and Secretary-General" (曾敏兴林吉祥蝉联民行党主席秘书职), 28 March 1977, p. 5.

[53] *Nanyang Siang Pau*, "DAP Representative Assembly Comes to a Close: Chen Man Hin and Lim Kit Siang Re-Elected as Chairman and Secretary-General" (民主行动党代表大会闭幕曾敏兴与林吉祥蝉联主席及秘书长), 18 December 1979, p. 6.

[54] *Sin Chew Daily*, "In Ipoh, Lim Kit Siang Accuses Chan Teck Chan of Neglecting Party Interests" (林吉祥在怡保指陈德泉目中无党), 16 March 1981, p. 6; Angela Tan, "Another DAP MP Is Axed", *The Star*, 17 March 1981, pp. 1 and 4; *Sin Chew Daily*, "Conflict in DAP Grows Ever Greater" (民行党政争风波越涌越大), 21 March 1981, p. 6.

[55] *Straits Times*, "DAP Exodus Hits Johore as 100 Quit Party", 20 March 1981, p. 15; *Nanyang Siang Pau*, "DAP Johor State Committee Organizes Emergency Meeting to Support Central Committee's Expulsion of Chan Teck Chan; On the Flipside, 13 Kluang and Mersing Branch Members Quit Party" (民行党柔州委员会紧急会议支持中央开除陈德泉另方面该党居銮及丰盛港支部13党员昨集体退党), 23 March 1981, p. 8.

members had eased their decision making.[56] Tensions between members of different linguistic backgrounds would not entirely dissipate, recurring in the following decade, albeit under altered conditions.

Concurrently, the national party's electoral calculations were changing, with downstream effects on DAP Johor. Rumours of an "unholy alliance" between the DAP and PAS circulated during the 1978 and 1982 general elections, wherein both parties purportedly entered into three-corner fights with the deliberate intention of splitting the BN vote. PAS was meant to absorb the Malay vote in non-Malay-dominant areas, whereas the DAP was to attract the Chinese vote in Malay-dominant districts.[57] In Johor, three parliamentary contests (Kluang, Muar and Tenggaroh) and seven state contests (Bandar Kluang, Bandar Maharani, Bekok, Mersing, Peserai, Serom and Tangkak) could have been part of this informal pact in 1978, decreasing to one parliamentary contest (Muar) and five state contests (Bandar Maharani, Bandar Penggaram, Bekok, Jorak, and Sri Lalang) in 1982. More transparently, though, in 1982, DAP Johor and Parti Sosialis Rakyat Malaysia (PSRM) signed an agreement to coordinate their candidatures.[58] In both situations, the DAP willingly took on the role of a practically Chinese partner, a major deviation from its initial thinking. It would take even more time for the party to develop this strategy fully, and to bring its members along with it.

---

[56] *Sin Chew Daily*, "Johor DAP Members Announce Party Departure Yesterday" (柔一批民行党员昨日宣布退出该党), 20 March 1981, p. 6.

[57] Diane K. Mauzy, "A Vote for Continuity: The 1978 General Elections in Malaysia", *Asian Survey* 19, no. 3 (1979), p. 290; Michael Ong, "The Democratic Action Party and the 1978 General Election", in *Malaysian Politics and the 1978 Election*, edited by Harold Crouch, Lee Kam Hing and Michael Ong (Kuala Lumpur: Oxford University Press, 1980), p. 164; Dilip Mukerjee, "Malaysia's 1982 General Election: The Tricky Triangulars", *Contemporary Southeast Asia* 4, no. 3 (1982): 301–15.

[58] *Sin Chew Daily*, "Johor DAP and PSRM Reach Electoral Agreement" (柔民行党人社党达致竞选协议), 5 April 1982, p. 8.

1985–99: STAGNATION WITH A BLIP OF REVIVAL

Song Sing Kwee, a lawyer by profession, joined the party in 1980.[59] He swiftly rose up the ranks and became the state chairman soon after taking over the position from Lee Kaw. His position as the chairman of DAP Johor received a significantly boost in 1986 when he was the sole elected opposition representative in Johor. In securing the state constituency of Bandar Maharani, DAP Johor successfully reversed their political fortunes in 1982 when they had failed to capture a single seat. Prior to his detention under the ISA in 1987 Operation Lalang, Song led protests in Johor on issues pertaining to illegal immigrants and the quality of Chinese teachers dispatched by the Education Ministry.[60] Song would lead DAP Johor until his abrupt resignation and departure in 1999.[61] From the mid-1980s to 1999, DAP Johor remained highly decentralized with party branches typically playing a larger role than the state or national party structure. This proved to be a major electoral disadvantage for the party, as explained in subsequent paragraphs. In the 1990s, the DAP failed to win any seats—whether state or parliament—in Johor save for the 1990 General Election (GE1990) when it entered a partnership with Dong Zong and other Chinese educational groups and secured a major electoral surprise.

The national collaboration between top leaders in the United Chinese School Committees' Association of Malaysia (Dong Zong) and the DAP served as a catalyst for DAP Johor in achieving political

---

[59] *Lianhe Zaobao*, "Who Has Been Arrested?" (谁被逮捕?), 28 October 1987, p. 2.

[60] *Lianhe Zaobao*, "Johor DAP Chairman Song Sing Kwee Arrested" (民行党柔佛州主席宋新辉议员遭警方逮捕), 29 October 1987, p. 21; *Lianhe Zaobao*, "Segamat Market Demonstration: Johor DAP Members Arrested" (昔加末公市前示威柔州民行党党要全数遭警方逮捕), 12 October 1987, p. 16.

[61] Ravi Nambiar, "DAP Strongman Song, Office-Bearers of Two Branches Resign En Masse", *New Straits Times*, 26 April 1999, pp. 1 and 4.

breakthrough in GE1990.[62] The alliance provided the DAP with crucial resources for grassroots mobilization in Johor, in addition to the entry of reputable Johor-based Chinese educationalists who stood on the party's ticket. Lim Fong Seng, then chairman of Dong Zong, prior to GE1990 had announced that numerous individuals from Dong Zong (himself included) were joining the DAP with the aim of creating a "Two Front System" in Malaysia.[63] Lim hoped that the collaboration would strengthen opposition forces in Malaysia and serve as a credible check against BN's hegemony.[64]

---

[62] Dong Zong is one of Malaysia's more influential CGA with a presence in all states and territories. Apart from serving as an umbrella body to facilitate coordination among Chinese-medium schools, Dong Zong also acts as a political pressure group in lobbying the government for Chinese-medium schools to receive better public funding and governmental recognition. Dong Zong has close collaborative relations with United Chinese School Teachers' Association of Malaysia (Jiao Zong), and both are collectively known as Dong Jiao Zong. See Dong Zong, https://www.dongzong.my/v3/en/about-us (accessed 24 June 2021).

[63] Lim first called for Chinese unity in 1981 to resolve the long-standing challenges faced by Malaysian Chinese and oppose the proposed educational reforms which were perceived as a threat to Chinese primary schools. Lim called the three Chinese-based parties—MCA, Gerakan and DAP—to set aside their political differences and pursue common goals instead, under the "Three-in-One" strategy. Since his calls went unheeded, Lim negotiated for Chinese educationalists to be admitted into Gerakan prior to GE1982. It was hoped that these individuals would champion Chinese educational interests from within the government. The latter after GE1982 was however reluctant to pursue such goals to the extent that Dong Zong had hoped for. Lim subsequently proposed a "Two Front System" for a united opposition front to compel the ruling government to resolve long-standing grievances over Chinese education. While the proposal failed to take off in GE1986, the proposal gained traction among top DAP leaders prior to GE1990. See Tan Yao Sua, "Political Participation and the Chinese Education Movement in Malaysia: The Role of Lim Fong Seng", Working Paper series 144/12, University Science Malaysia Center for Policy Research and International Studies, 2012.

[64] *Sin Chew Daily*, "Lim Fong Seng and 27 Others Join DAP" （林晃升等27人加入行动党), 19 August 1990.

Under the terms of collaboration, several of Dong Zong's top leaders took up DAP membership and contested as candidates for the GE1990. Lee Ban Chen, upon relinquishing his post as executive secretary of Dong Zong, contested for the Bakri parliamentary seat in Johor.[65] In Johor, the national alliance also spurred leaders of Chinese schools who were not part of Dong Zong to contribute to the DAP. Lim Wan Show, board member of Muar Chung Hwa High School, contested for Bandar Maharani (a state seat within Bakri) as a gambit to strengthen the party's campaign to wrestle Bakri parliamentary seat from the MCA.[66] Lim would successfully defeat the MCA for the Bandar Maharani state seat in GE1990. Ng Wei Siong, Kluang Chung Hwa High School board member and a committee member in a local Chinese business organization, contested for the Kluang parliamentary seat.[67] The collaboration with the DAP extended beyond leaders of Chinese schools, and had spillover impact on other CGAs. In Johor Bahru, Chan Jock Lan responded to the call made by Lim Fong Seng and led five members from Johor Bahru Chinese Federation – Youth to join the DAP.[68] The collaboration between CGAs and the DAP in GE1990 was a watershed moment since it was the first instance where prominent Johor CGA leaders provided public endorsement to the DAP.

The collaboration was likely to have boosted the party's profile among Johorean Chinese, as the CGA members were well regarded in that community. Lee Ban Chen and Chan Jock Lan, among others, organized political discussion lectures and forums across Johor during

---

[65] *Sin Chew Daily*, "One Is Duty-Bound to Participate in Politics" (参政参选义不容辞), 19 August 1990; Tee Beng Lee, "A Place Fought on Ordinary Civilian Politics" (平民政治争一席), *Oriental Daily*, 3 May 2013.

[66] Tee, "A Place Fought on Ordinary Civilian Politics".

[67] *Lianhe Zaobao*, "Lim Fong Seng Leads 26 Men to Join the DAP" (林晃升率领26人加入民主行动党), 19 August 1990, p. 21.

[68] Ibid.; *The Rocket*, "Democratic Fighter Chan Jock Lan in Southern Johor" (柔南巾帼争民主，铿锵玫瑰詹玉兰), March 2016.

the run-up to GE1990, which attracted sizeable turnouts.[69] Forums served as an effective tool to outreach and engage voters, in addition to the traditional mode of election campaigns and vote canvassing. In addition to Kluang and Bakri, individuals from Chinese schools also assisted in the campaign efforts for constituencies contested by Gagasan Rakyat (GR).[70] GR was an election pact established prior to GE1990 between the DAP, Semangat 46 (S46), and the Malaysian People's Party to avoid three-cornered fights between opposition parties. S46 had been formed in 1989 by Tengku Razaleigh and other UMNO members who had resigned from UMNO.[71] Chan and her teammates from Johor Bahru Chinese Federation – Youth campaigned for S46 in Johor Bahru, as the parliamentary seat was contested by Jaafar Onn from S46.[72]

The DAP-S46 opposition alliance may have resulted in some Johorean Malays being more inclined to vote for a DAP candidate in constituencies where the latter contested. DAP Johor did secure an unprecedented victory and best-ever performance by clinching three state constituencies in GE1990, namely Maharani, Bekok and Jementah. The DAP victories in Bekok and Jementah were particularly unexpected, since both were widely seen as safe deposit seats for the MCA. Pang Hok Leong, the DAP candidate for Bekok, was expecting a defeat and was "shocked" when his election victory was announced.[73]

---

[69] *Sin Chew*, "300 Participants Attended the Dong Zong-DAP Dialogue on Amendments to the Education Act" (行动党与董教总举行教育修正令对话), 7 June 1990; Chan Jock Lan, personal correspondence, 15 January 2021 and 8 February 2021.

[70] Wong Peng Sheng, personal correspondence, 21 January 2021.

[71] The schism in UMNO occurred as Tengku Razaleigh led "Team B" to challenge the "Team A" led by then Prime Minister Mahathir Mohamad.

[72] Chan Jock Lan, personal correspondence, 15 January 2021 and 8 February 2021.

[73] Soo Wern Jun, "Small Boy' Pang Ready to Challenge for the Big Prize of Labis", *Free Malaysia Today*, 5 May 2018.

The collaboration between the DAP and Chinese educationalists was not to last, partly due to diverging opinions on GR partnership between the DAP CEC leadership and the Chinese educationalists in the lead-up to GE1995.[74] There were also divisions within DAP Johor, though this was not a contributing factor towards the eventual parting of ways between the DAP and the CGA individuals at the national level. The factionalism within DAP Johor became apparent soon after GE1990, when Ng Wei Siong resigned from his position as the deputy chairman of DAP Kluang joint committee in 1991.[75] The decision for Ng to contest in the Kluang parliamentary seat was decided by the CEC, but this was not well received by Lim Kwi Siam and Khoo Ching Ong who were respectively the chairman and secretary of DAP Kluang joint committee.[76] Lim Kwi Siam and his brother Lim Kwi Ho were prepared to contest for the parliamentary and state seat in Kluang, but the entry of Ng prior to GE1990 scuttled these plans. Lim Kwi Siam would eventually stand in Paloh (a state seat in Kluang) while his brother did not contest. 1990 was the first—and last—election for Ng Wei Siong, Lee Ban Chen and Lim Wan Show. The DAP would fail to retain any of the three seats in 1995, nor succeed in capturing any new seats.

DAP Johor had inherited the decentralized style from the 1970s and continued to operate in a similar fashion during the 1980s to 1990s, with party branches as the primary agents tasked to organize outreach activities, grassroots mobilization and election campaigns. The decentralized structure proved to be a major handicap for the party in Johor in the 1990s.

Unlike UMNO or MCA, DAP did not have a strong grassroots presence in Johor despite efforts since the 1970s to expand its presence

---

[74] See Tan Yao Sua, "Political Participation and the Chinese Education Movement in Malaysia", pp. 18–19.

[75] *Lianhe Zaobao*, "Ng Wei Siong Quits Kluang DAP Post" (同其他党要不咬弦吴维湘辞居鑾民行党党职), 12 April 1991, p. 13.

[76] *Nanyang Siang Pao*, "Ng Wei Siong Resigns from Party Positions" (吴维湘辞行动党职), 12 April 1991; *Sin Chew Daily*, "Key Personnel in DAP Johor Resigns" (居鑾行動黨黨要吳維湘辭職), 12 April 1991.

by establishing new branches. At first glance, the party made significant progress as the number of branches increased from around thirty in the 1970s to almost eighty in two decades.[77] A significant number of branches, however, failed to satisfy ROS regulations in conducting branch elections, and were not legally recognized as active.[78] Only twenty branches, or one-quarter of the total number, were active in 1999.[79] Typically, only the active branches organized outreach activities and had a presence on the ground during the campaign period.[80] In addition, most grassroots members served on a part-time and ad hoc basis since they had their full-time jobs and did not receive compensation for party-related work.[81] The number of electorates for each state seat was about 20,000 to 30,000 during the 1990s. Without a sizeable mass of grassroots volunteers to build up rapport among residents, DAP candidates in Johor faced an uphill task to capture seats. A typical DAP election rally would only attract twenty to thirty attendees.[82]

In contrast, BN had a formidable grassroots machinery in Johor with one branch in almost every village or urban housing estate. The MCA had a strong presence in new villages while UMNO was dominant in rural and semi-rural Malay areas.[83] Unlike the DAP, both the MCA and

---

[77] *Sin Chew Daily*, "13 DAP Branches in Johor Passed Resolution for Song Sing Kwee to Resume Party Position" (柔行動黨13支部議決要求恢復宋新輝黨職), 18 March 1999.

[78] Gan Peck Cheng, personal correspondence, 22 December 2019.

[79] Nambiar, "DAP Strongman Song, Office-Bearers of Two Branches Resign En Masse".

[80] As DAP contested around ten Johor state seats in both GE1995 and GE1999, on average a candidate only had the support of *two* branches to assist in vote canvassing. While the party's membership in Johor stood at around 5,000 during the same period, the number of active DAP members was similarly estimated to be significantly lower than the figures above, considering the large number of inactive branches.

[81] Wong Peng Sheng, ibid.

[82] Boo Cheng Hau, personal correspondence, 14 November 2020.

[83] Ng Yak Howe, personal correspondence, 15 November 2020.

UMNO possessed well-oiled grassroots resources for door-to-door house visits and vote canvassing.[84] In the initial decades after its establishment, MCA Johor developed extensive networks with Chinese CGAs and much of these ties continued through the 1990s.[85] Up till 1983, all MCA Johor chiefs were Chinese-speaking businessmen apart from Lee San Choon who served from 1973 to 1977.[86] Wong Shee Fun and Chua Song Lim were both prominent businessmen who held important leadership posts within the Chinese organizations in Johor. As Chinese associations remained influential in community, the close collaboration with MCA helped tilt the political scale towards MCA.

In addition, the MCA pivoted towards constituency services in the aftermath of GE1990 with the establishment of the MCA Public Service and Complaints Bureau. To address criticisms that the party was ineffectual in eliminating bumiputra preferential policies, the MCA increasingly took up the mediator role starting from the 1990s where officials petitioned on the residents' behalf to government agencies.[87] These requests typically concerned municipal services and appeals for governmental permits. Through the provision of constituency services, elected MCA representatives and aspiring candidates built up rapport with residents in their constituency.[88]

Apart from the weak mobilization of grassroots, DAP Johor also lacked the financial resources for a well-oiled election campaign machinery. The burden of raising funds for election campaigns fell upon DAP branches, as the national party did not provide financial resources

---

[84] Chew Peck Choo, personal correspondence, 20 November 2020.

[85] Boo Cheng Hau, ibid.

[86] The chairperson of the state liaison committee served as the state MCA chief. Wong Shee Fun (1949–61), Chua Song Lim (1961–73) and Teo Ah Kiang (1977–83) were all businessmen. See Lee and Chan, *Electoral Politics and The Malaysian Chinese Association in Johor*, pp. 10–12.

[87] James Chin, "New Chinese Leadership in Malaysia: The Contest for the MCA and Gerakan Presidency", *Contemporary Southeast Asia* 28, no. 1 (2006): 72–73.

[88] Boo Cheng Hau, ibid.

to the branches.[89] Some of the common election expenses included production and distribution of publicity materials (e.g., pamphlets and flags) and setting up a venue for rallies. Fund-raising dinners—conducted on an annual basis—were the main sources of revenue for DAP branches.[90] Each attendee for the fund-raising dinner would contribute between RM30 and RM50, with the bulk of the proceeds channelled towards the party branch.[91] However, reception towards DAP fund-raising dinners were typically lacklustre and DAP grassroots had to sell the tickets through painstaking door-to-door visits in the community.[92] The institutional arrangement where branches were responsible for fund-raising and financing election campaigns played out less effectively in Johor, compared to Selangor or Penang where DAP branches generally had a larger pool of supporters for donations. DAP branches in Johor were typically cash-strapped up till the 2000s.[93] An absence of adequate finances would have likely compelled DAP candidates in Johor to scale back on their campaign expenses, with an adverse impact on their electoral performances.

The party suffered a further setback for the 1999 General Election (GE1999), as state chairman Song Sing Kwee abruptly resigned as state chairman in the lead-up to the election due to disagreements with national DAP leaders.[94] His departure triggered resignations from several DAP Johor branch leaders, including Pontian and Penerok branches.[95]

---

[89] Chew Peck Choo, ibid.

[90] Chan Jock Lan, ibid.

[91] Chan Jock Lan, ibid.; Hew, *A Study of DAP: Beyond Dogmatism and Pragmatism*, p. 220.

[92] Chan Jock Lan, ibid.

[93] Tan Chen Choon, personal correspondence, 21 January 2021.

[94] Nambiar, "DAP Strongman Song, Office-Bearers of Two Branches Resign En Masse"; *New Straits Times*, "Fiery Meeting Deepens DAP Crisis", 7 March 1999, p. 3.

[95] Nambiar, "DAP Strongman Song, Office-Bearers of Two Branches Resign En Masse".

Figures 1 and 2 highlight the sharp drop in the vote share and votes casted for DAP in GE1995 and GE1999.

The departure of Song was a significant setback for the DAP in Johor. In addition to the vacuum in top leadership, the resignation of DAP branch leaders in the state also weakened the party's morale.[96] As the incident was widely publicized in mainstream newspapers, its credibility among Johorean voters also took a hit. Pang Hok Liong took over as acting DAP Johor chairman and led the party into GE1999.[97] However, the results proved disastrous for the DAP; it failed to clinch a single state or parliamentary constituency in Johor. The dismal performance in two consecutive general elections in 1995 and 1999 served as a catalyst for DAP Johor to embark on a process of reforms and renewal.

Ironically, the vacant state chairman post afforded DAP Johor the opportunity to reset its leadership and chart a new course of action.

EARLY 2000s: RECOVERING FROM THE DISASTROUS ELECTORAL PERFORMANCE IN THE 1990s

Shortly after the electoral defeat in GE1999, the national party leadership chose Ahmad Ton as the new Johor state chairman, taking over from acting chairman Pang Hok Liong. Ahmad Ton was well regarded in DAP Johor for his multicultural attitudes.[98] He became the first non-Chinese to assume the post of DAP chairman in Johor. Prior to that, he had held key leadership positions in DAP Johor and actively stood as candidate for previous general elections. Ahmad Ton served as DAP Johor chairman from 1999 to 2001, and was succeeded by Pang Hok Liong in 2001. Pang served until 2005, after which Dr Boo Cheng Hau took over.

---

[96] Ravi Nambiar, "Johor DAP Looks Set for More Trouble", *New Straits Times*, 27 April 1999, p. 4.

[97] Gan Peck Cheng, ibid.

[98] Song Sing Kwee, personal correspondence, 19 November 2020 and 23 November 2020.

Figure 1: The DAP Vote Share in Johor (Percentage Terms) between GE1969 and GE1999

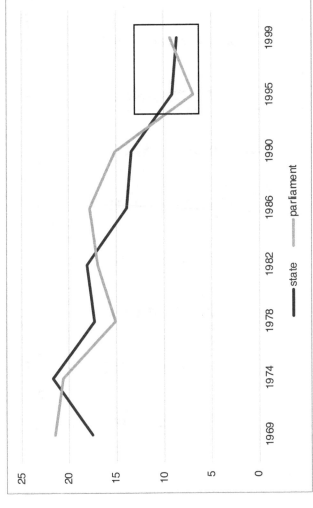

Source: Elections in Malaysia: A Handbook of Facts and Figures on the Elections 1955–1995 (Kuala Lumpur: New Straits Times Bhd); *Almanak Keputusan Pilihan Raya Umum: Parlimen & Dewan Undangan Negeri 1959–1999* (Kuala Lumpur: Anzagan Sdn Bhd).

Figure 2: Number of Votes Cast for the DAP in Johor between GE1969 and GE1999

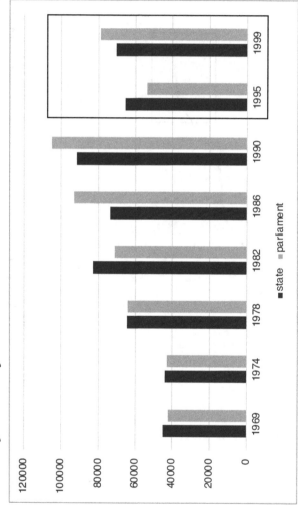

Source: Elections in Malaysia: A Handbook of Facts and Figures on the Elections 1955–1995 (Kuala Lumpur: New Straits Times Bhd); Almanak Keputusan Pilihan Raya Umum: Parlimen & Dewan Undangan Negeri 1959–1999 (Kuala Lumpur: Anzagan Sdn Bhd).

DAP Grassroots Activities and Constituency Services in Skudai and Bentayan

In the early 2000s, the DAP branches in Skudai organized open house events to coincide with the various ethnic celebrations, for instance Mid-Autumn Festival, Hari Raya and (at a later period) Deepavali.[99] DAP Socialist Youth (DAPSY), under the leadership of then DAPSY Johor chief Dr Boo in the early 2000s, collaborated with the Skudai branches in holding these events. As open house events were conducted once every few months, the sustained interactions enabled DAP members to build up familiarity with the residents in contrast to the previous engagement method of fund-raising dinners which are held only once a year. By celebrating the festivals of each major ethnic group, DAP Skudai grassroots and DAPSY members could outreach to residents from diverse races while illustrating the party's commitment to champion the interests of all Malaysians.

Apart from open house events, DAP Skudai branches were also actively involved in community welfare projects since the early 2000s with active involvement from the grassroots including Taman Ungku Tun Aminah branch led by Chan Jock Lan. These welfare schemes were customized to tackle specific needs of Skudai residents, which enabled residents to believe that the DAP leaders were genuine about creating an impact in their everyday lives.

A significant portion of Skudai residents worked in Singapore and commuted daily, often returning home late in the night with their children left to their own devices. A youth centre was established in Skudai during the early 2000s which offered tuition to students at a minimal fee, staffed by DAP Johor grassroots members and volunteers.[100] The centre also offered counselling services for at-risk and delinquent youths. As most DAP volunteers were not trained in counselling, in the subsequent years delinquent youths were paired up with a religious organization located

[99] Chan Jock Lan, ibid.

[100] Tan Hong Pin, personal correspondence, 11 May 2019.

in Skudai which offered free and professional (secular) counselling services.[101] Dr Boo also utilized his clinic in Skudai for social welfare services, by charging low-income patients a nominal amount.[102]

Due to the emphasis on outreach programmes since the early 2000s, the DAP began to attract a sizeable number of volunteers (non-party members) and grassroots (registered party members) particularly in Skudai and Bentayan. Up till the 1990s, most grassroots members in DAP Johor were veterans from blue-collar backgrounds.[103] The entry of younger Malaysians and white-collar professionals starting in the early 2000s resulted in a renewal of the grassroots machinery, as these professionals used their expertise to improve outreach activities and campaigns.[104] For instance, white-collar professionals could effectively articulate the party's agenda through speeches in election rallies and a deft use of messaging.[105] As Johoreans became more interested in contributing towards DAP grassroots activities, DAP candidates in GE2008 benefited from a better-resourced election machinery to conduct campaigns and outreach.

Dr Boo, as the chief of DAPSY Johor and subsequently (from 2005 onwards) as DAP Johor chairman, managed to rope in some students and fresh graduates of Universiti Teknologi Malaysia (UTM) located within Skudai as volunteers. One of them was Tan Hong Pin, who subsequently persuaded a group of his UTM friends to similarly contribute to these activities.[106] Tan would later rise within the ranks of DAP Johor and serve as EXCO in the Johor state government during Pakatan Harapan's tenure.

Constituency services refer to the act where representatives of a political party—usually grassroots members or volunteers—appeal

---

[101] Ooi Cheng Chai, personal correspondence, 4 February 2021.

[102] Ibid.

[103] Ng Yak Howe, ibid.; Song Sing Kwee, ibid.

[104] Wong Shu Qi, personal correspondence, 14 November 2020.

[105] Ng Yak Howe, ibid.

[106] Ooi Cheng Chai, ibid.

to the relevant government agencies on behalf of a resident.[107] These appeals typically concern municipal issues and governmental permits. As elected state or parliament representatives are usually seen as the agent responsible for the provision of constituency services, most requests had been processed by the UMNO or MCA Johor representatives. Despite its status as an opposition party without even an elected Johor state or parliament representative, the DAP began operating full-time service centres in Skudai and Bentayan (Muar) in the early 2000s.[108] During the back-and-forth process of liaising with the relevant authorities while keeping the resident updated, a sense of goodwill was formed. Constituency services therefore served as a crucial avenue for prospective election candidates to establish rapport while becoming familiar with community needs ahead of the next general election. In addition, the DAP grassroots members also demonstrated their competency in negotiating with government agencies, despite being in the opposition.

GE2004 showed early signs that the transformation within DAP Johor was bearing fruit. Even though the party failed to capture any state or parliamentary seat in Johor, it came close, and lost DUN Bentayan and Skudai only by a narrow margin of 3 per cent and 8 per cent, respectively. This was a sharp reversal from GE1999 for Skudai; a comparison is unavailable for Bentayan as the seat was created only in GE2004.

State-Level Leadership and Structural Reforms

During the 1990s, there were several notable and publicized incidences of dispute within DAP Johor regarding the candidate selection for general elections. Some of these disputes occurred at branch level, for instance between Lim Kwi Siam and Ng Wei Siong in the Kluang branch. Other disputes concerned state leaders and party branches, for instance, in GE1995 when party chairman Song Sing Kwee attempted to stand in the

---

[107] See Meredith L. Weiss, "Duelling Networks: Relational Clientelism in Electoral-Authoritarian Malaysia", *Democratization* 27, issue 1 (2020): 100–18, https://doi.org/10.1080/13510347.2019.1625889

[108] Tan Hong Pin, ibid.

Segamat parliamentary seat despite opposition from the Segamat DAP branch.[109]

To forestall similar situations from occurring in the future, in the lead-up to GE2008, a candidate selection committee was established. This committee was tasked with interviewing potential candidates to determine their suitability based on whether the person had cultivated a local presence among the branch members and the residents in the constituency he/she is intending to contest.[110] However, final approval would still be made by the DAP CEC rather than the selection committee. The creation of this committee benefited the party twofold. Firstly, it served as a mediator to resolve disputes within party branches regarding candidate selection and to de-escalate conflicts during the lead-up to general elections. Secondly, it ensured that candidates chosen to represent the DAP had a credible presence among grassroots members and residents in the constituency, which increased the likelihood of victory. It also encouraged aspiring candidates to cultivate the ground over a sustained period, rather than being selected for the mere sake of contesting or as last-minute candidates as had been the case in previous elections in some constituencies.[111]

The discourse among DAP grassroots members also experienced a transformation after Dr Boo took over as state chairman in 2005. During the 1990s, the general sentiment among DAP Johor grassroots members was to oppose and fight the incumbent BN government.[112] Upon assuming the state chairman post, Dr Boo established a clear goal for the party to be in government within two decades (i.e., by 2025).[113] Grassroots members were encouraged to adopt the mindset of a constructive opposition force, building the party to eventually replace BN as the governing party.[114]

---

[109] *Sin Chew Daily*, "Missteps by DAP: Jementah and Bekok at Risk of Defeat" (行動黨犯兵家大忌，利民達彼咯難守), 12 April 1995.

[110] Tan Chen Choon, ibid.

[111] Ramakrishnan Suppiah, personal correspondence, 15 November 2020.

[112] Gan Peck Cheng, ibid.

[113] Tan Chen Choon, ibid.

[114] Ooi Cheng Chai, ibid.

Instead of merely criticizing the government's policies, DAP grassroots members were encouraged to brainstorm and bring up feasible policy alternatives. In contrast to the previous decade when outreach and engagements were ad hoc, Dr Boo also stressed the importance for grassroots members to be in frequent contact with the residents.[115] Dr Boo utilized his own connections with leaders of CGAs for the DAP grassroots to gain a platform to engage with these organizations. Through his medical practice, Dr Boo also gained contacts and built relations with Johor Bahru residents.[116] While the ties established between DAP Johor and CGAs in the 1990s were limited to a handful of organizations, the party took an intentional effort to establish ties with a broad range of CGA and community agencies (including religious groups) starting from the early 2000s. As DAP Johor established relations with CGAs during the 2000s, the influence which MCA once wielded within these agencies subsequently waned.

2008–13: GROWING FROM STRENGTH TO STRENGTH IN JOHOR

In the 2008 General Election (GE2008), the DAP surpassed its previous record made in GE1990 when it captured four state seats and one parliamentary seat. It also marked the start of an exponential rise for the DAP in Johor over the coming decade. Interestingly, except for Mengkibol, the remaining three seats were won in GE2008 by a comfortable margin of at least a few thousand votes. Dr Boo defeated his BN opponent in Skudai by a margin of 13,000 which was (until then) the largest winning margin an opposition candidate had ever garnered in Johor.

Using Skudai state constituency as a case study since it has been one of the seats with the greatest involvement by DAP Johor in terms of

---

[115] Tan Chen Choon, ibid.

[116] Ooi Cheng Chai, ibid.

welfare and grassroots activities, one may conclude that support for DAP had risen over the past two decades among both the Chinese and Malay electorate. As seen from Figures 3 and 4, the support for DAP among all polling districts (Pusat Daerah Mengundi) in Skudai had broadly risen in each election cycle. There was a significant increase in support for DAP among polling districts (PDM) where ethnic Malays comprise about 35 to 40 per cent of the electorate (Figure 4), from a 40 per cent vote share in GE2004 to a 60 per cent vote share in GE2013 (and somewhat higher for GE2018). One may estimate the vote share in GE2008 to have been at least around 50 per cent in this group of polling districts, considering the 13,000 large margins of victory. Nonetheless, DAP continued to perform somewhat better in polling districts where ethnic Chinese constitute more than 80 per cent of the electorate as seen in Figure 3.

BETWEEN GE2008 AND GE2018

The achievements made in 2008 by the DAP in Johor, with the benefit of hindsight, marked the start of a decade-long rise. In GE2013, DAP captured four parliamentary seats and thirteen state seats in Johor. GE2018 ended six decades of BN regime, with the DAP winning in all the six parliamentary and fourteen state constituencies it contested in the state except for the Ayer Hitam parliamentary constituency (see Figures 5 and 6).

Starting from the 2011 Tenang by-election, the state and national leadership became more active in coordinating and implementing a statewide Johor election strategy.[117] Ramakrishnan Suppiah, a Selangor member of the DAP, was tasked by the national leadership to serve in Labis during the 2011 Tenang by-election. He spent the next two years building up the local grassroots machinery and building relationships with Labis residents.[118] He was selected to stand as DAP Labis parliamentary candidate in GE2013. Cultivating a Malay or Indian candidate in constituencies where non-Chinese electorate constituted

---

[117] Liew Chin Tong, personal correspondence.

[118] Ramakrishnan Suppiah, ibid.

Figure 3: Polling Districts in Skudai, Johor: Ethnic Chinese Composition and the DAP's Vote Share

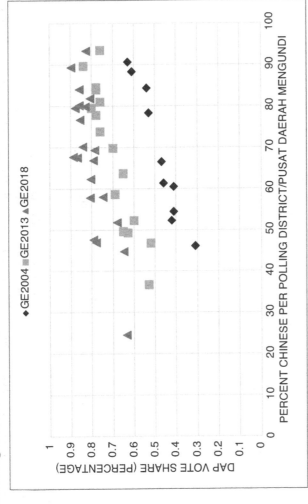

Note: Each square/triangle/diamond represents one polling district. The ethnic breakdown data for GE2008 Skudai polling district (PDM) is unavailable. The ethnic breakdown data for GE2018 Skudai polling district are based on data updated on December 2017. There is a 1 per cent discrepancy in population number between December 2017 and GE2018.
Source: Authors' calculation based on data provided by Ong Kian Ming, SPR Malaysia, Attorney General Chambers, PKR, Tindak Malaysia.

Figure 4: Polling Districts (PDM) in Skudai, Johor: Ethnic Malay Composition and DAP's Vote Share

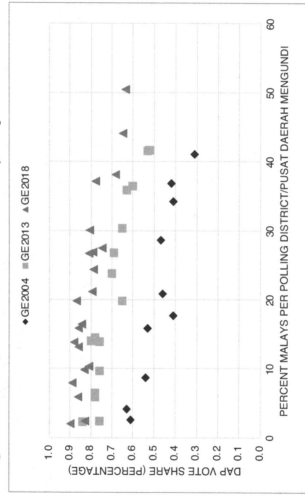

Note: Each square/triangle/diamond represents one polling district. The ethnic breakdown data for GE2008 Skudai polling district (PDM) is unavailable. The ethnic breakdown data for GE2018 Skudai polling district are based on data updated on December 2017. There is a 1 per cent discrepancy in population number between December 2017 and GE2018.

Source: Authors' calculation based on data provided by Ong Kian Ming, SPR Malaysia, Attorney General Chambers, PKR, Tindak Malaysia.

Figure 5: Number of State Seats Contested and Won by the DAP in Johor since 1969

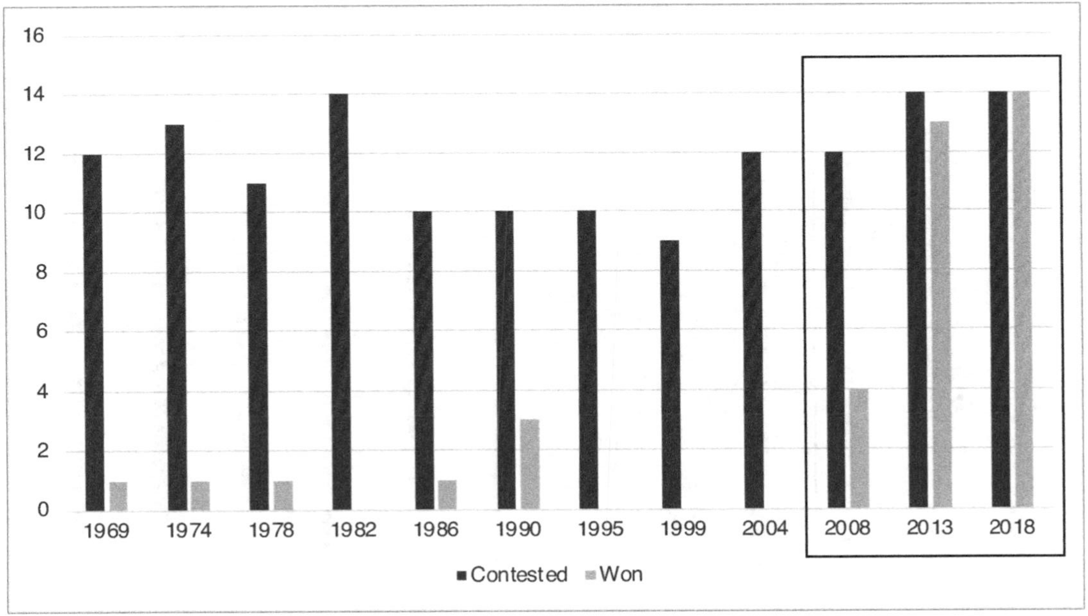

Figure 6: Number of Parliament Seats Contested and Won by the DAP in Johor since 1969

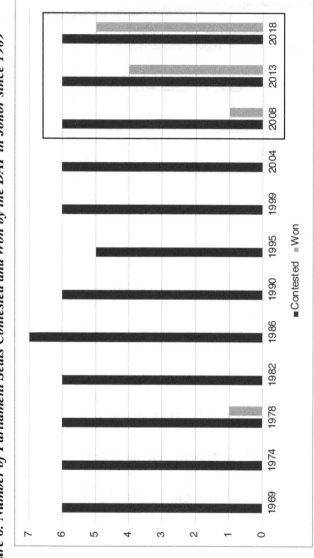

a sizeable share may be interpreted as a sign to the electorate that the DAP was active in championing the interests of all Malaysians. Labis has the highest percentage of Indian voters among all the parliamentary constituencies in Johor, at 15 per cent. Even though Ramakrishnan lost to MCA Chua Tee Yong in GE2013 by a slim margin of fewer than 400 votes, the outcome was a sharp contrast to the 4,000 majority votes Chua obtained in GE2008 against DAP candidate Teo Eng Ching.

In a departure from past practices where DAP candidates in Johor were typically chosen from among Johorean members of the party, GE2013 saw the entry of top DAP national leaders to contest for parliamentary seats in the state. Party veteran Lim Kit Siang stood in Gelang Patah (renamed Iskandar Puteri in GE2018). His entry was widely perceived as a sign that the party had shifted its focus to Johor, and possibly contributing to DAP's rising popularity among Johoreans in GE2013. Teo Nie Ching who contested in Kulai was a DAP Member of Parliament from Selangor. In addition to retaining Bakri, DAP wrestled Gelang Patah, Kulai and Kluang from BN in 2013 (Figure 9). The coordination between the state and national leadership further intensified and picked up pace when Liew Chin Tong took over from Dr Boo as state chairman in 2014. Interestingly, all the four parliamentary seats which DAP won were in semi-urban areas while the party failed to capture the rural seats of Labis and Tanjong Piai (Figures 7 and 8).

The DAP made a clean sweep of the fourteen states seats it contested in 2013, except for Paloh (Figures 9 and 10). It also managed to wrestle a few rural state constituencies from BN, including Jementah and Bekok. Most gains in state seats were concentrated in urban and semi-urban areas, especially in and around Johor Bahru.

Despite the entry of well-known national leaders from other states, and the remarkable gains made by DAP, its allies in Pakatan Rakyat (predecessor of Pakatan Harapan) fared less well. The Malaysian Islamic Party (PAS)—then part of the Pakatan Rakyat (PR) coalition before its departure in 2015—and People's Justice Party (PKR) won only four and one state seat, respectively, in Johor. Johor remained solidly behind BN as it won thirty-eight out of the fifty-six state seats.

The turning point came in GE2018. Pakatan Harapan (PH, a reconfiguration of PR and now including the National Trust Party

Figure 7: *Parliament Seats Won by the DAP in Johor since GE2008*

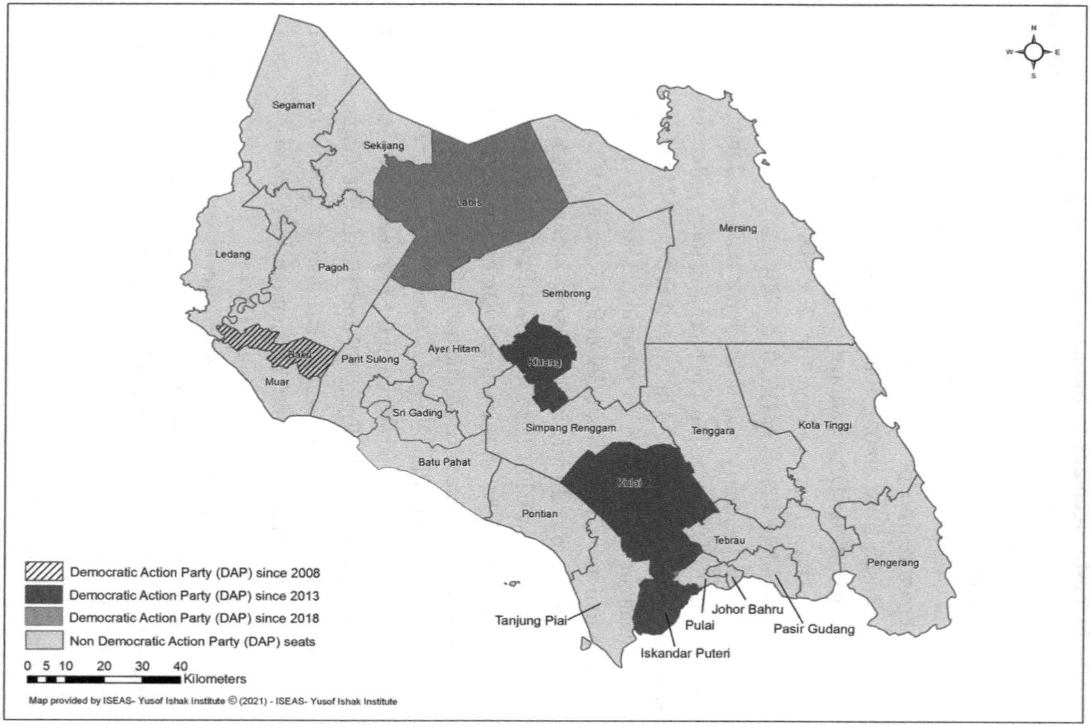

Figure 8: Distribution of the Chinese Electorate in Johor Parliamentary Seats, Based on the 2018 Electoral Boundaries

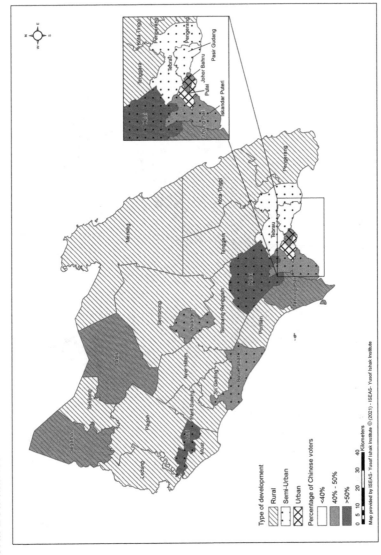

Type of development
- Rural
- Semi-Urban
- Urban

Percentage of Chinese voters
- <40%
- 40% - 50%
- >50%

0 5 10   20   30   40
Kilometers

Map provided by ISEAS - Yusof Ishak Institute © (2021) - ISEAS - Yusof Ishak Institute

Figure 9: *State Seats Won by the DAP in Johor since GE2008*

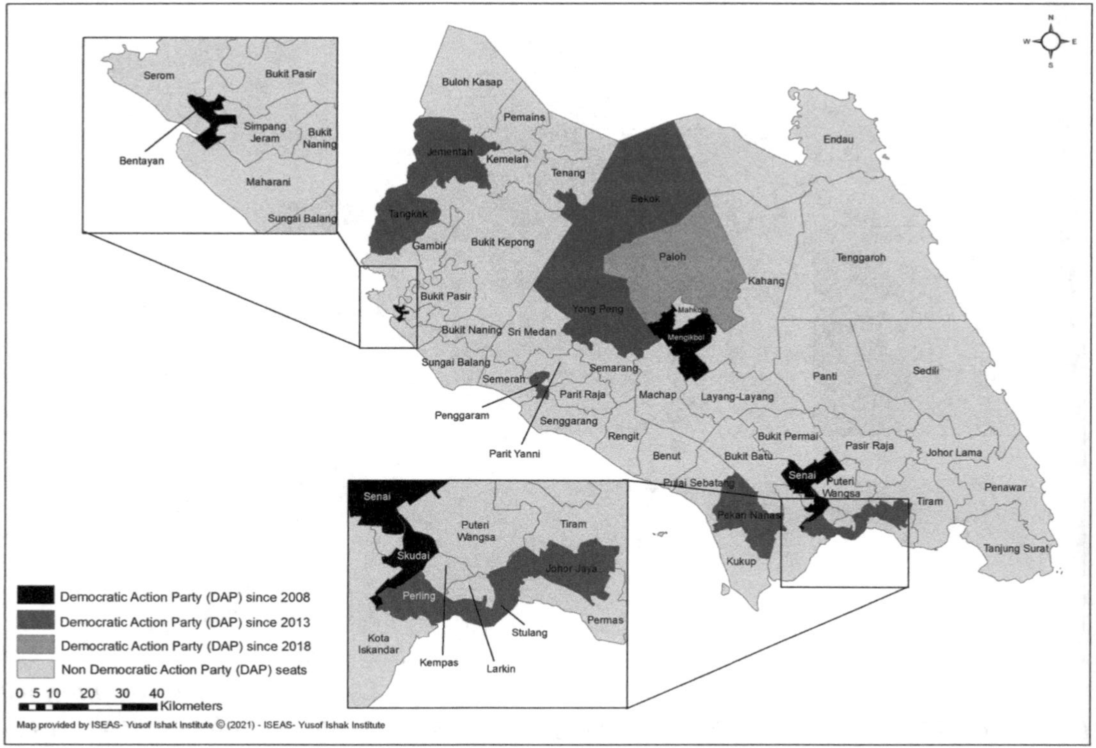

Democratic Action Party (DAP) since 2008
Democratic Action Party (DAP) since 2013
Democratic Action Party (DAP) since 2018
Non Democratic Action Party (DAP) seats

0 5 10   20   30   40
Kilometers

Map provided by ISEAS- Yusof Ishak Institute © (2021) - ISEAS- Yusof Ishak Institute

Figure 10: Distribution of the Chinese Electorate in Johor State Seats, Based on the 2018 Electoral Boundaries

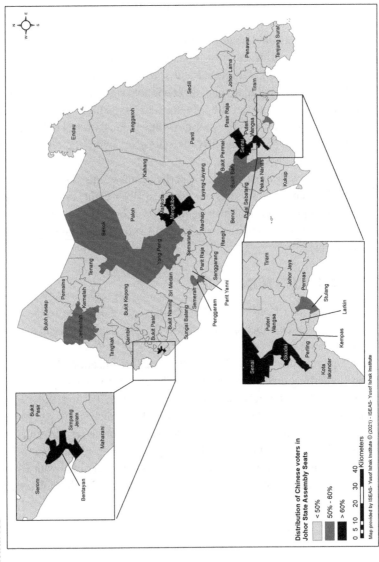

[Amanah] and PPBM), alongside DAP and PKR, contested as a united front, and scored a massive victory in Johor.[119]

The DAP contested in the exact same fourteen seats as it did in 2013. It managed to wrest Paloh from BN—the sole state assembly seat it lost to BN in 2013—and achieved a clean sweep of all the fourteen states seats it contested. In contrast to GE13, the other component parties in PH now scored an unexpected and spectacular victory, with Amanah, PPBM and PKR winning nine, eight and five state seats, respectively. In winning thirty-six out of the fifty-six state assembly seats in Johor, the PH thus replaced BN as the state government in 2018. BN only managed to win nineteen (out of the fifty-six state seats), with the remaining one being won by PAS.

PH also won most of Johor's parliamentary seats. The PH coalition won eighteen of these seats compared to BN's eight; this was the best result an opposition had ever achieved in Johor. The DAP, on its part, retained the four seats it won in GE2013 and gained Labis as well (see Figure 11).

CONCLUSION

Johor had long been regarded as the bastion of BN due to the unique historical and developmental legacy of the state. But that began to change two decades ago.

Up until the 1990s, DAP Johor was organizationally weak with an under-resourced grassroots machinery. Consequently, the party was unable to replicate its success in Selangor, Penang and Perak in the state. Most of the electoral gains in Johor during the party's early years were concentrated around Kluang, due to the resourcefulness of early DAP leader, Lee Kaw. The party had a blip of success in Johor during the GE1990 when DAP at the national level allied with Chinese educationalists Dong Zong, which saw the entry of well-known figures

---

[119] PAS left the PR coalition in 2015. PPBM would quit the PH coalition in February 2020 during the Sheraton Move.

Figure 11: Parliament Seats Won by PR/PH in GE2013 and GE2018

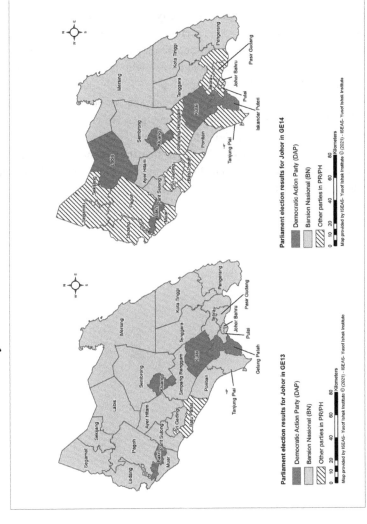

Parliament election results for Johor in GE13

■ Democratic Action Party (DAP)
▨ Barison Nasional (BN)
▧ Other parties in PR/PH

0 10 20   40   60   80
▬▬▬▬▬▬▬▬▬▬ Kilometers

Map provided by ISEAS-Yusof Ishak Institute © (2021) - ISEAS-Yusof Ishak Institute

Parliament election results for Johor in GE14

■ Democratic Action Party (DAP)
▨ Barison Nasional (BN)
▧ Other parties in PR/PH

0 10 20   40   60   80
▬▬▬▬▬▬▬▬▬▬ Kilometers

Map provided by ISEAS-Yusof Ishak Institute © (2021) - ISEAS-Yusof Ishak Institute

as candidates for the party and a significant boost from the movement's grassroots machinery. However, this success was short-lived, and the collaboration with the Chinese educationalists collapsed by GE1995.

During the 2000s, DAP Johor began to undergo significant reforms, with changes to its leadership and party structure, as well as a doubling down on grassroots and social welfare activities, particularly in Skudai and Bentayan. A more successful coalition among opposition parties had also been developed at the national level, with the DAP as a key player. These efforts showed signs of paying off in GE2008 when the party achieved its (until then) best performance in Johor. By GE2013, DAP Johor had emerged as a formidable contender. However, as a whole, the Pakatan Rakyat coalition did not perform well enough to topple the state government. It was only in GE2018, that the reconfigured opposition coalition, now called Pakatan Harapan, managed to wrest the Johor state administration from BN for the first time.

Appendix 1: List of Interviewees

Due to the Movement Control Order (MCO) implemented in Malaysia, the interviews since March 2020 were conducted through online platforms.

No.	Name	Date and Time
1	Boo Cheng Hau	14 November 2020, 14:30–15:10
2	Chan Jock Lan	15 January 2021, 14:00–14:55 8 February 2021, 18:00–18:30
3	Cheo Yee How	18 November 2020, 10:00–11:30
4	Chew Chong Sin	23 December 2019, 14:00–15:00
5	Chew Peck Choo	20 November 2020, 16:00–16:30
6	Gan Peck Cheng	12 January 2019 22 December 2019, 14:30–15:30
7	K. Siladass	11 November 2018 24 November 2020, 15:00–15:40
8	Lee Kaw	11 November 2018 19 November 2020, 16:00–17:30
9	Ng Yak Howe	15 November 2020, 10:00–10:45
10	Ooi Cheng Chai	4 February 2021, 16:15–17:30
11	Ramakrishnan Suppiah	15 November 2020, 13:15–13:45
12	Song Sing Kwee	19 November 2020, 14:15–15:15 23 November 2020, 14:45–16:00
13	Tan Chen Choon	21 January 2021, 20:00–21:00
14	Teo Nie Ching	6 January 2021, 11:30–12:00
15	Wong Peng Sheng	21 January 2021, 11:00–11:30
16	Wong Shu Qi	14 November 2020, 15:30–16:10

Appendix 2: DAP Johor Electoral Contest Results (1969 to 2018) by Parliamentary and State Constituency

https://docs.google.com/document/d/1itPmBI9GhrUrV5XaXtEHCVib GN3-wz23JI0sjZTv_yo/edit?usp=sharing